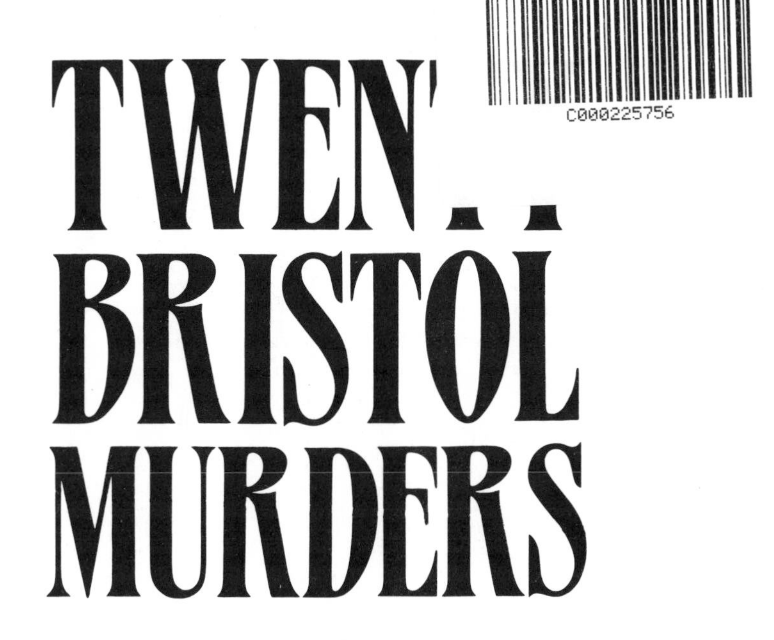

Veronica Smith

REDCLIFFE
Bristol

First published in 1992 by
Redcliffe Press Ltd
49 Park St, Bristol.

ISBN 1 872971 67 9

British Cataloguing-in-Publication Data.
A catalogue record for this book is available
from the British Library.

Typeset and printed by
The Longdunn Press Ltd., Bristol.

Contents

Introduction

There are some who would condemn my fascination with the subject of murder on the grounds it shows a degree of ghoulishness and morbidity in my character but I would defend that criticism. It is not so much the gruesome aspects which hold me in thrall but rather the events leading up to the tragedies, the personalities of killer and slain and the wondrous domestic detail gleaned from contemporary reportage, in particular the evocative accounts recorded by Victorian journalists.

I must admit I often identify so closely with the female victims that I can almost re-enact the circumstances under which their lives ended. When I was working with Chris Selby of the *Evening Post* once, doing the location pictures for the Ada James story I became so graphic in my details of her last fatal steps as we walked down Narroways Hill that he finally said: 'Are you sure you're not Ada reincarnated?'

I can sense Amelia Deacon's frustration as she screams insults at her ne'er-do-well husband and Elizabeth Spear's fury when she discovers John has pawned her gowns in order to buy liquor. Poor Mary Lewis walking unknowingly to her death resplendent in her new shawl and bonnet and Ellen Hayball's small daughter playing blissfully with her beads on the sunlit doorstep, totally unaware that her mother lay dead in an upstairs room – it is such minutiae which capture my imagination and, I trust, that of my readers.

My aim in writing this book has been to bring to life the players in these sad, forgotten little dramas. I hope I have succeeded.

I should like to thank: the very patient staff in the Reference section of the Central Library for manhandling dozens of bound editions of old newspapers on my behalf; my uncle, Lionel Ellery for his continued encouragement; my stepmother, Poppy Peck, for her constructive criticism; my friends Sue Lee, for taxi-ing me around on the trail of old photographs and Hayley Goodwin for her help in typing my sometimes undecipherable handwriting; my daughter Mandie Britton for researching the Mason's Arms murder; my apprentice, Daley Lawrence for assistance on the College Green killing; Mike Tozer for his superb photographs, Sheena Stoddard (City Museum and Art Gallery) for tracing old prints; Pam Dickson landlady of the Mason's Arms, Stapleton for loan of the photograph, the *Bristol Evening Post* for allowing me access to their files particularly Gerry Brooke the Librarian and Features Editor Jim Keay for his initial help in establishing my writing career and to all my friends for their continued enthusiasm for my efforts.

This book is dedicated to the memory of my mother Violet Peck (née Ellery) who instilled in me my love of history.

Credits

The pictures on pages 7, 11, 32, 42, 51, 54, 59 and 69 are reproduced by kind permission of the City of Bristol Museums and Art Gallery.

The photographs on pages 12, 15, 18, 36, 39 and 49 are reproduced by courtesy of the M.J. Tozer Collection.

Murder on the Winding Path

The year was 1855. The papers were full of news of British victories in the Crimea, but for many Bristolians life just carried on as normal.

The Avon Gorge looked very different from today's scene. It would be a decade before Clifton Suspension Bridge was opened.

And, on the Hotwells side of the river, in place of Bridge Valley Road, there was a cliffside quarry owned by a Mr Eglestaff, surrounded by a huddle of cottages for his workers with a hostelry known as The Rock Beerhouse.

Further up the Gorge, on the edge of Clifton Down, was Cook's Folly Tavern, which served superior ales. It was to this inn that nine-year-old Melinda Payne was sent one August Saturday evening to fetch a quart of beer for her father, who worked as a carpenter at the quarry.

She was dressed in a brown frock and a garden bonnet and carried a ginger-beer jar for the ale. She clutched a sixpence in her little hand.

Melinda started up the winding path at 6.30 p.m. She had run the errand before and it was estimated the round trip would take her the best part of an hour.

On the way she met her brother, George, returning from work and asked him for a ha'penny to buy biscuits.

When Melinda did not return after an hour, George was sent to look for her.

At the tavern, the landlady told him that Melinda had collected the ale and had been given two little cakes.

George rushed home, but no Melinda awaited him. The entire family, carrying lanterns and candles, searched the cliffside until after midnight, but found nothing.

Exhausted, they returned home, intending to resume their search at first light. The only reported sighting of the girl was by Thomas Kingsworn, a young donkey driver, who told her father that he had seen a child answering the description walking towards the Sea Walls, with her jar and, thinking it contained water, asked her for a drink.

It was 12-year-old George who found her body at 7.30 the following morning, the face 'smothered in blood' from dreadful injuries inflicted on her head. She also had knife wounds to her throat. The corpse was in a rocky hollow at the rear of a cottage inhabited by Samuel Handy, a labourer, his wife Elizabeth and their children. Stones had been piled over the body, which lay with one arm raised as though to ward off blows. Fragments of the cakes were found nearby, but no ale jar.

An Inspector Attwood took charge of the case and had the body removed to the Rock Beerhouse to await the inquest, which opened the following day at the Rownham Tavern, during which the child's wounds were described in grim detail.

She had not been sexually assaulted. It was thought she had not been killed on the spot where she was found, as all the occupants of the Handy's cottage denied hearing a struggle.

Meanwhile, a bloodstained knife had been discovered by two young men. It had been hidden in rocks by the zig zag path. The ginger-ale jar was found some 50 yards further up in the woods. James Payne, the girl's father, was closely questioned, as a bloodstained shirt had been found in the family's cottage but there was an explanation for this – he had had an accident at work on the Friday.

His wife, who had five other children, vouched for the fact that he

A nineteenth century view of Cook's Folly where little Melinda was last seen alive.

was at home at the relevant time.

William Skinner, a quarryman who lodged with the Paynes, told police that he had returned from work at about 7.15, had heard the parents instructing George to search for Melinda, then had himself set off for Bristol.

So who was responsible for the frenzied attack on little Melinda?

The alibis of the family appear watertight, although it is possible they closed ranks to protect one of their members. The lodger? Could he have waylaid her? If so, why?

The young donkey driver is the only person who admitted to seeing her after she had left the tavern.

Although initially he had told her father he had spoken to her, when giving evidence he said that at about 6.45 p.m., he had met a little girl with a jar coming from the direction of Cook's Folly. There was, he said, 'company in the carriage and some others sitting on the wall. I was sitting on the box. I did not speak to the girl, nor she to me, nor did I see or hear anyone else speak to her.' Payne was quoted as remarking after the discovery of the body that: 'It's no stranger did that', and saying something to the effect that she was killed for a quart of beer.

Whom did he suspect? Or was this a red herring and information given to a Sgt Phillips that Payne had been seen going up the gully that fateful night between 6 and 7 o'clock true?

Poison from a Real Charmer

Mary Ann Burdock was quite a character. A country girl, from a village near Ross-on-Wye, she was a buxom, fresh complexioned, 19-year-old when she arrived in Bristol in the 1820s.

She presented herself at the Hiring Fair and was rapidly selected by Mr Plumley, a poulterer who conducted business from premises in St Nicholas Street. But he caught her with her fingers in the early nineteenth century equivalent of the till and he dismissed her without a reference. Had industrial tribunals been in force in those days she would have lodged an appeal. Instead she hired a solicitor to sue for what would, in modern day parlance, be termed "wrongful dismissal."

The wheels of justice ground as slowly in those days as they do today and by the time the case came even close to approaching court she had grown tired of waiting and had married Mr Agar, a tailor. But she fast became bored with life as a tailor's wife and took off with the Lord Mayor's coachman, setting up house with him in The Horsefair.

She was obviously a charmer who was very attractive to men and her next conquest was a wealthy wine merchant. During the relationship she managed to acquire sufficient capital to rent a house in Limekiln Lane which she ran as a brothel.

Local antipathy eventually persuaded her to abandon the scheme but by this time she had seduced a man by the name of Wade, a steam packet steward. Together they set up a lodging house in Trinity Street, St Philips. When he died she married one of the lodgers, Mr Burdock. She rented one of her rooms to Clara Smith, the widow of an Old Market ironmonger, who had what in those days amounted to a considerable sum of money. Mary Ann focused all her attentions on her new lodger who was plagued with a racking cough. Her devotion paid off. Soon the vulnerable widow had placed her life savings in her landlady's hands. About £500 of this cash was put to immediate use to pacify impatient creditors. More money was needed, though, and Mary Ann was desperate.

She sent her husband out to buy two penn'orth of arsenic which was administered to the ailing Clara Smith in hot milk at bedtime.

When the remains of Clara Smith were interred in St Augustine's churchyard in the winter of 1834, Mary Ann believed her troubles were at an end. But she had reckoned without the intervention of Mrs Smith's nephew and nieces, and she had also overlooked Mary Allen, an undernourished young servant girl in her employ. Mary Allen testified to having witnessed her mistress pouring yellow powder into the widow's drink. The body was exhumed and found to contain a fatal dose of arsenic.

Mary Ann Burdock was arrested and stood trial at the Guildhall. She was found guilty and sentenced to hang. She remained cool, however, even under sentence of death. She checked out the measurements of the coffin with the carpenter and stipulated it must be 'full-sized and flannel lined.' She needed, she explained, 'a comfortable shroud.'

It rained on April 15th, 1835, the day of her execution, when 50,000 spectators turned out to witness the event. Dressed in black silk she began her walk to the gallows. She was asked if she required an umbrella. 'No need to bother now,' Mary Ann replied, 'I shan't be wearing this lot again.'

Mary Ann Burdock.

A watercolour drawing by T.L.S. Rowbotham of Limekiln Dock with Brandon Hill in the distance. Mary Ann Burdock rented a house near the dock.

Hounded to Death

In April 1803 John, youngest child of ex-seaman Thomas Horwood and his Orkney-born wife, was born in their Hanham cottage. He was the last of their ten children. Coal-mining was the principal industry in the district at that time and the sons all went to work down the pit. One son, Joseph, was injured in a pit accident when he was 15 and the following year his twin brother James met his death underground when a roof caved in. In view of this John was never very happy about pursuing this line of work but stuck it for two years until an opportunity came up for him to enter the employ of Philip George at his Spelter works.

Cottages at Hanham at the turn of the century.

Up to this point the stocky, rather short, fair-skinned youth had been industrious and chapel-going but around the time of his sixteenth birthday he became involved with a group of young people in the locality, an event which was to bring about his eventual downfall. The chief attraction of this clique was, for John, Eliza Balsum a girl some 18 months older than himself. He became so besotted with her that he abandoned all pretence of working so that he could spend every available moment in her company.

He tricked his parents into buying him clothes on the pretext of needing them when seeking employment and turned to petty theft to provide ready cash. On one instance he and Eliza's brother were apprehended and sentenced to a short spell in prison.

Whether Eliza was initially attracted to John Horwood is not clear but certainly by the end of 1820 he was making her life sheer misery by his obsessive behaviour. He hounded her relentlessly, making 'indelicate and improper' suggestions to her and even went so far as to threaten her life. Once he vowed he would burn down her parents' house. His frustration reached a crescendo at Christmastide that year when he waylaid her in a lonely Hanham lane and flung vitriol over her. Luckily she was unhurt although the acid burned the clothes she wore.

Understandably, after this terrifying incident she became extremely nervous and when she saw him hanging about her home a few weeks later she ran indoors and her family chased him off. Defeated by the sheer weight of numbers, Horwood fled, shouting back as he did so: 'The first time I catch her I will mash her bones small as ashes.' Shortly afterwards Eliza's friend, Hannah Fry, heard him declare 'If I catch her with another man I will be the death of her.'

At the end of January 1821 Horwood spied Eliza one evening on the hillside near her cottage. He was with his cronies, Joseph and William Fry and Thomas Barnes. Eliza was in the company of Joseph Reece and William Waddy. Horwood's group was about 36 yards away from Eliza and the two lads when he stooped and picked up a large stone which he flung at her with all his might. It hit her on the right side of her head and she fell into a brook she was crossing, pulling William Waddy down with her. The party carried her home and her mother put her to bed. She was in a great deal of pain and suffering from vomitting attacks and when, after three days, no improvement could be detected in her condition she was taken to hospital.

Horwood was unrepentant. 'If she don't die there when she comes out I'll be damned if I don't kill her,' he announced callously, adding 'If I was to hear her say I hove the stone I would crack her bloody nose.'

The stone had caused a depressed fracture of Eliza's skull and she died in the Infirmary on Saturday, 17th February.

In the meantime John Horwood had been arrested one dawn by the Sheriff's Yeomen, Officers Bull and Sew. He had tried to escape through his bedroom window but it was too narrow and had then resorted to violence, fighting off his captors on the stairs with a quarryman's hammer. Sensing defeat was imminent he flung the hammer at Bull but fortunately the blow was minimal and Horwood was overcome and borne away to his victim's bedside where the deposition was read to him. He showed total indifference to the damage he had done and when asked if he had any questions to put to Eliza he said 'No'. The dying girl was too upset to even glance in his direction throughout the proceedings.

Horwood went on trial for murder, was convicted and sentenced to death at the New Gaol in Cumberland Road. In the days leading up to his death he became grateful for the comfort of religion and said, 'Lord, thou knowest that I did not mean then to take away her life but merely to punish her: though I confess that I had made up my mind, some time or other, to murder her.'

Horwood went to the gallows on Friday, 13th April 1821, three days after his eighteenth birthday. He left behind a verse which was printed and sold on the day of execution. It reads:

JOHN HORWOOD IS MY WRETCHED NAME
AND HANHAM GAVE ME BIRTH
MY PREVIOUS TIME HAS BEEN EMPLOYED
IN RIOTING AND MIRTH.

ELIZA, OH ELIZA DEAR!
THY SPIRIT, OH, IS FLED!
AND THY POOR MANGLED BODY LIES
NOW NUMBER'D WITH THE DEAD.

CURS'D IS THE HAND THAT GAVE THE BLOW
AND CURS'D THE FATAL STONE
WHICH MADE THY PRECIOUS LIFE BLOOD FLOW
FOR IT HAS ME UNDONE.

The Man with a Fatal Attraction

Of all the shopping thoroughfares in Bristol perhaps the one which has changed least over the years is Gloucester Road on and around Horfield Common. Of course the trades represented have altered with the times – for example No 389 is now the BRW Video Library. But in the summer of 1908 it was a rather second rate antiques shop. The proprietor was newly arrived in the West country. His name was George Joseph Smith.

The Muller Road end of Gloucester Road where George Smith traded in antiques.

Immediately upon opening the business in July he advertised for a housekeeper at a salary of £16 per annum. There was only one applicant – 28-year-old Edith Pegler who lived with her mother at 368 Gloucester Road. Smith proposed marriage within a week and the wedding took place on July 30th. Edith was unaware that her husband already had one legal wife and another whom he had bigamously wed.

She was similarly oblivious to the fact that her new husband had served a prison sentence for incitement to robbery and that he was adept at persuading gullible women to hand over to him their life savings. Descriptions of Smith draw attention to his hypnotic eyes.

During their seven-year marriage Edith was frequently left in charge of the shop while George was away on business. Unknown to her this business involved adopting an alias, scouring popular resorts for likely victims whom he married. Having got his hands on their cash he returned to Bristol and the faithful Edith.

One such prey was Bessie Mundy from Warminster whom he wooed and won at Weymouth in August 1910. As soon as her money was in his possession he did his disappearing act, writing to the innocent spinster to the effect that he'd caught a sexual disease from her and would be away for a long time having expensive treatment.

Eighteen months later this unscrupulous man encountered Bessie on the promenade at Weston-super-Mare. Amazingly, she greeted him rapturously and a reunion was effected. Hastily penning a note to Edith explaining he was departing for Canada on business, he whisked Bessie off to Herne Bay, where he arranged for them to have their wills witnessed.

He then marched her off for a medical check up with the story that she had suffered an epileptic fit. The doctor called two days later and could find no evidence of this but prescribed some simple remedy. The third time the doctor was summoned the matter was more serious. Bessie had drowned in her bath. It had happened, said Smith, while he was out buying fish for their breakfast.

A verdict of accidental death was returned. After a brief return to Edith's loving arms the man with the fatal attraction was off again. This time his hunting ground was Southsea and the formula was repeated with Alice Burnham, a chubby 25-year-old nurse. She died in a similar fashion to Bessie on her honeymoon in Blackpool.

He was back in Bristol for Christmas where he was described as being 'the life and soul' of Edith's mother's party. Early in the New Year he and Edith moved to Cheltenham but the following winter found him back in Bristol and paying court to Margaret Lofty a 38-year-old clergyman's daughter whom he met on the Downs.

They were married in Bath on December 17th, 1914. The same plan was swiftly put into action during their London honeymoon. After drowning her he sat at the organ in the parlour of their lodgings playing "Nearer my God to Thee".

He was more subdued on his return to Edith that Christmas. The inquest on Margaret Lofty had been adjourned. Smith's luck was running out, particularly as the *News of the World* ran a headline

"Bride's tragic fate on day after wedding."

Alice Burnham's family read the story, made the connection, contacted the police and the man dubbed by the press as the "Brides In The Bath Murderer" was arrested on February 15th. His trial at the Old Bailey attracted capacity crowds and he was executed on Friday, 13th August, 1915.

Death in the Afternoon

Whit Sunday, 1899. The day dawned fine and warm and Bristolians all over the city packed up picnics and set off on outings.

In Jones Court, a cluster of diminutive dwellings off Avon Street, at a little after 1 p.m., Laura Silks made her way to number four, the home of her friend and neighbour, Ellen Hayball.

The evening before when they had met at 7 p.m. Ellen had been in an agitated state. Her husband Fred had not yet returned from his work on the docks and she announced she was going to find him and 'get some money off him'. It seems she was in very little doubt that Fred's wages were rapidly filling some landlord's pocket.

As they parted Ellen asked Laura to call round on the Sunday at midday as she wished to discuss her husband's ill-treatment of her. She had also hinted that she was endeavouring to terminate an unwanted pregnancy and was considering using an empty house in the court for the purpose.

From her window during the course of that Sunday morning, Laura had observed Fred collecting several buckets of water from the communal pump in the court. He was later to be seen preparing vegetables at the sink. Of Ellen there was no sign but her little girl sat on the step playing with some beads.

At 1 p.m. Fred left the house and Laura proceeded to keep the promise she had made to her friend. She walked into the three roomed cottage but Ellen was neither in the kitchen nor the living room. With, perhaps, the thought of the impending miscarriage in her mind, Laura decided to try the bedroom. She pushed open the door then froze as she was confronted with the sight of Ellen's body slumped on the floor in a pool of blood. She had been savagely beaten about the head and part of one ear had been completely hacked away.

Laura rushed from the house and sought out another neighbour, Mrs Jenkins. Together the two women went in search of help and encountering PC White on his beat they brought him to view the grisly scene. While the constable was examining the corpse and noting the newly-washed hatchet in the back kitchen Laura and Mrs Jenkins decided to seek out Fred.

He was obviously a creature of habit as they made straight for the "Cross Guns" in Temple Street. Laura must have been a mistress of understatement. She informed Fred that his wife was 'apparently dead' and that he should go home immediately. Fred made a laconic remark to the effect that he intended to finish his drink first so the two women returned to Jones Court. The last that was seen of Fred was a figure crossing St Philip's Bridge.

The inquest opened at Bedminster Police Station on May 25th. From evidence given here it was revealed that the Hayballs had five

Temple Street at around the time of Ellen Hayball's murder. The Cross Guns Tavern stood opposite these buildings.

children, only two of whom lived at home. The eldest was in the Guardian House in Cumberland Street, another had been adopted by a couple called Long, while the third lived with an aunt.

Fred and Ellen's 11 years of married life together had been far from happy ones. Ellen's sister Minnie Pocock who lived at Brook Street, Bedminster, in answer to the Coroner's query 'Did you know anything about the circumstances leading to your sister's death?' replied: 'It was not more than I have expected these last four years. But I always made up my mind to hear of it at night between 11 and 12 or 12 and one o'clock, not in the daytime. I could write out a history about her life.' Minnie went on to reveal that soon after the marriage Fred had been jailed for 14 days for wife-beating and assaulting his mother-in-law and he and Ellen had lived apart for three years afterwards. They effected a reconciliation but the following year he received a three-month sentence for an attack on her. He was released on a Saturday morning and that very evening he battered her again.

Six weeks before her death Fred had launched another violent attack on Ellen, kicking her in the head. He had failed to appear in court to answer the resultant summons, saying to her 'If I thought you was going up against me I would out with a knife and cut your throat now.'

On being asked why her sister always went back to such a brutal man Minnie explained, 'She was a woman very quick to forgive and, of course, she thought of the little children.'

PC James Smith was called to give evidence at the resumed inquest and he described his encounter with Ellen Hayball at 11.15 p.m. on the night before her death. She had approached him in Avon Street. She was holding a child in her arms and she showed him her bruised hand, telling him her husband had accused her of consorting with other men.

All-in-all it was a sorry tale which emerged of poverty, drunkenness and violence. One can only conjecture at the sequence of events during the final hours of her life. Evidence indicated she had been hacked to death as she lay in bed. Perhaps when Fred finally arrived home she reiterated her threat to take him to court again. If she did it was an unwise remark to make to a drunken man with an aggressive temperament.

So what became of Frederick Hayball, the 37-year-old ex-sailor, stout and clean shaven, last seen crossing St Philip's Bridge attired in black patched jacket, white and blue spotted muffler, soft cap and moleskin trousers? He was never seen again. Rumour had it for a time that his was the body fished out of the dock a few days later but this theory of suicide turned out to be unfounded – the body was not his.

Mrs Vera Moore of Coalpit Heath, who first related the tale to me, told me that her aunt, Ginny Prankard, lived in Jones Court at the time of the murder and was a witness to the ghastly discovery, a memory which was to haunt her all her life. There was no doubt in the minds of Ellen's family and friends as to the identity of her slayer.

Mrs Moore showed me a copy of the memorial card which her father always kept. It reads: In loving memory of Ellen Scudder Hayball, who was murdered by her husband on May 21st 1899, aged 32 years.

Like a flower in bloom cut down in its prime
Leaving her motherless children behind
How wretched her life quickly it passed
She clung to her husband until the last
Like a bird with its wings he very soon fled
Leaving the poor creature on the floor quite dead
How sweet to rest upon that shore
When pain and sorrow are no more

Interred in family grave, Redfield Chapel, West, Undertaker, Narrow Wine Street, Bristol.

'Go and May You Perish . . .'

When Amelia Hallett aged 27 wed Edward Deacon, a rather overweight shoemaker six years her junior, she must have thought she was, at last, settling down to a life of reasonable happiness if not total marital bliss. She was a somewhat stout woman with a slight deformity who worked at her home in St James Barton as a tailoress to support herself and her 12-year-old illegitimate daughter, Ann. Whatever hopes she may have cherished, however, were soon to be shattered, for the following autumn Edward disappeared from her life not to return for a further five years.

Amelia seemed to view his defection philosophically, continuing to earn her own living as before, enlisting, in due course, the help of young Ann. She also took in a lodger, Matilda Bryant, to help make ends meet.

One wonders at her reaction when Edward re-entered her life just before the Christmas of 1875. He approached his estranged wife with caution, first testing the water by making contact with Ann. He made a fairly substantial financial contribution initially as a means of buttering up Amelia and, at first, the reconciliation appeared to be a success. It was not long, though, before Edward began to revert to his old ways and on Saturday nights when he had partaken more than his share of liquor the quarrels reached a crescendo.

On Sunday, 20th February 1876 a squabble from the previous night continued unabated. During the course of that day Edward threatened Amelia that the next time he hit her she would end up in the Infirmary and that he 'would be locked up for it'. Ann, by now a young woman of 18, was sufficiently alarmed by all this to take the axe they used for wood chopping and hide it in Matilda's room.

On the Monday Edward did not go to work, spending the day instead visiting his favourite haunts. He returned that evening very much the worse for wear to face, naturally enough, further recriminations from his wife.

Harmony was still not restored the following morning, by which time Edward was suffering the effects of his over-indulgence and could not stomach the breakfast Amelia had prepared for him. In true bout-drinker's fashion he was feeling very hard-done-by on this chill morning and he confided to Matilda that he and his wife 'could not live comfortably'. He proceeded to pack some lunch in a handkerchief, announcing that he was leaving town.

Amelia, meanwhile, had left the house to visit a neighbour. She returned after Edward's departure and steadfastly set to work on her sewing machine. Ann had also left the house, going about her business of obtaining a fresh supply of outwork from a nearby shop. On her return she found Edward once more in occupation, his threats mere idle ones made out of self-pity and probably an attempt to draw attention to himself. During the course of the morning Edward managed to patch things up with Amelia and, together with Matilda, they adjourned for a drink at the Star Inn. The tranquillity was not to last, however. When Ann came back to 8, Barton Street in the late afternoon with two friends, Frank Silvester and Frances Johnstone, Edward declared, 'It's a lucky job you've come back, you've saved your mother's life.'

He then struck out at his wife and, as Ann intervened, Frances berated him for his harsh treatment of Amelia. This seemed to subdue Edward and Silvester later testified they were on 'friendly terms' when he left the house. On being questioned regarding the adjective 'friendly' he enlarged, 'They were not swearing at each other.'

The reign of peace must have been very brief for soon afterwards Edward went next door to the house of his neighbour, Mary Lockstone, with a request to borrow a hatchet to chop some wood. Within minutes of his return to number eight Mary heard appalling groans emanating from the Deacon residence. She sped round to the back of their house but finding the door locked she ran to the front and banged loudly on the door. When Edward opened it she demanded, 'For God's sake, Deacon, what have you done?' He simply said, 'Go and see' and walked off into the twilight. Mary hurried through to the kitchen and found Amelia lying on the floor, her head in the coal hole, the hatchet beside her. Blood flowed profusely from head wounds. Mary unlocked the back door and screamed out to Jane Coghlan whose house in Barton Court backed on to the Deacons'. Jane took it upon herself to set off in pursuit of Edward while Mary enlisted medical aid for the dying woman.

Edward was heading in the direction of the upper Arcade when Jane spotted his stocky form in the gathering gloom. She ran to catch him up and grabbed him by the arm saying, 'You've killed your wife.' He told her he was on his way to give himself up but Jane was taking no chances on him escaping. He was not entirely sober but far from drunk. Perhaps the awareness of the awful deed he had done had lessened the effect of the alcohol in his bloodstream.

In the meantime Amelia had been transported to the Infirmary but had died of her injuries en route. She had five hatchet wounds to the head, two of which were so savage they had penetrated her brain.

At the subsequent trial the question was debated as to whether the charge should be manslaughter or murder. It appears the catalyst which sparked off Deacon's frenzied attack was Amelia's words 'Go and may you perish like the stones in the street'. It took a mere ten minutes deliberation on the part of the jury to decide on a verdict of 'Guilty of murder' and the hot-tempered shoemaker was hanged on April 24th, 1876.

Murder by the "Mason's Arms"

The little village of Stapleton was shocked to the core one Saturday afternoon in September 1836 with the discovery of a woman's body in Lypiatt's Lane. The wife of labourer Robert Davis who lived in a nearby cottage came home at about quarter to three and told her husband there was a woman lying in the lane either dead or drunk. Together with two friends, Bridgeman and Long, he went to investigate. He found the woman with blood seeping from her head. Her shawl and gown had been removed and her white straw bonnet lay on the ground nearby. Her gloves were pulled down over her hands. It was soon established that the woman had died of gunshot wounds. Indeed, shots had been heard earlier but it was thought someone had been shooting blackbirds. Her body was taken to the "Mason's Arms" and laid out for the public to view in an attempt to identify the mystery female.

The annual fair held at St James' Barton had just closed and Mary Tickle who travelled with one of the shows was among those who came to look at the corpse. 'Good God!' she gasped 'This is Mrs Bartlett's mother.'

The Mrs Bartlett to whom she referred was Sarah, the young wife of Charles Bartlett, a handsome 23-year-old leading man of Inglestone's San Pareil Theatre company who had been performing at the Fair.

Elizabeth Beresford, landlady of the Mason's Arms and her assistant Sarah Light recognised a face in the crowd. They were sure it was the man they had seen the preceding Saturday in the company of an older woman, whom they now realized must have been the deceased.

Elizabeth Beresford recalled that the woman had been attired in a white straw bonnet, a light coloured dress and a dark shawl with a patterned border. The pair drank gin and water, she remembered and stayed only a short while, about 15 to 20 minutes. She confided that the man had appeared to be in some manner peculiar.

He had been a little more forthcoming with Sarah Light and after talking about the Fair asked her the way to Winterbourne. His companion asked how far it was to Oldbury Court and told Sarah that she lived in Monmouth. The woman then remarked that she did not know whether it was altogether proper for her to go out with the young man as she had not known him long.

When they left Sarah accompanied them to the door and watched them cross the road and go into the lane. This puzzled her as she thought they were making for Winterbourne and the lane did not lead in that direction.

The Mason's Arms, Stapleton.

The man they had identified as the deceased's companion was Charles Bartlett who had come to the inn to confirm that the body was that of his mother-in-law. Bartlett was taken into custody and his rented appartments were searched. The search uncovered a horse pistol, which did not appear to have been recently discharged, and a pocket pistol, double-barrelled, about 6 or 7 inches long with a spring bayonet. There were traces of gunpowder in the pocket of some trousers and in a coat pocket. In his waistcoat pocket was a stick, about 6 inches long, rounded to fit the barrells of the pistol. It appeared blackened as if by gunpowder.

Henry Lovell a young lad of about 15, also a member of Inglestone's entourage, was questioned by the police and he described how Bartlett had sent him out for ammunition the Friday before. He had said to Henry 'If my wife asks you what you are going for, say for some caps.' Bartlett's explanation for this was that he used the guns as part of his act.

Meanwhile Mr Holloway, a surgeon, had examined the body of the deceased whose name was Mary Lewis and found at least 12 shots had been fired at close range to her head. Four had lodged in her brain. Evidence was mounting against the young actor.

Charles and Sarah had been married a mere two months when the tragedy occurred. She was 18 when she wed Bartlett and before her marriage her father handed over a £47 dowry to her fiancé, explaining that no more money would be forthcoming until her mother's death.

It seems that from the outset Bartlett made every attempt to cultivate the favour of Mary Lewis. Ten days earlier the two of them had travelled to Bath where she had business and apparently some transaction took place in connection with a robbery charge against Bartlett. The full details relating to this dealing never came to light at the inquest together with other reports 'that could not, without great impropriety, be mentioned at the present stage of this tragical affair.'

The victim, a seemingly lively lady in her fifties had appeared in fine fettle on that fateful day she met her death. She had left her lodgings at about 11.00 a.m., next to be seen near the "Black Swan" at Eastville at midday in the company of Bartlett. They were spotted by Thomas Cook, a Winterbourne hatter and erstwhile drinking companion of Bartlett's.

That evening Sarah and Charles, together with some show-business friends, the Melburys, called at Mary's lodging house where her landlady told them she had not seen Mary since mid-morning. Sarah said she had been expecting her mother to come to tea that day but she hadn't turned up.

Charles Bartlett was taken in custody and at the initial enquiry he requested three witnesses, Mr Mitchell, Mr Melbourne and Mrs Stock, be called to provide him with an alibi but the coroner advised him against doing so. Bartlett, however, ignored this counsel and insisted they be called but only Mrs Stock appeared. She deposed that she had seen him between noon and one o'clock on the fateful Saturday. She was not explicit as to where she had seen him but apparently it was at her house where Bartlett and his wife were lodging. She had seen Mrs Lewis on a couple of occasions and saw her at 11 o'clock on that day. Again she did not specify where she saw her.

Charles Samuel Bartlett was charged with wilful murder and held in custody until the following April when he came to trial. He pleaded 'Not Guilty' but the jury were not convinced and he was sentenced to death. On hearing this, Sarah went into premature labour and gave birth to a still-born child. She did, however, express satisfaction at the verdict and was heard to declare her husband had slain her mother 'for the money'.

One is left wondering how on earth Bartlett hoped to get away with his crime. He behaved with extraordinary stupidity by shooting her in broad daylight within minutes of leaving a public house in her company. He compounded the error by returning to the Mason's Arms to identify the body, although this issue may have been forced on him by Mary Tickle's testimony. Was the motive money or were there other factors which did not emerge at the trial? How close was his relationship with Mary Lewis and what was the true story regarding the robbery charge? These questions seem unanswerable but one is left with intense sympathy for poor young Sarah losing mother, child and husband in such a short space of time and under such horrific circumstances.

Stroll Ended in Cold Blood

Work over for the day, the girls spilled out of the nail and button factory in St James' Square. Hurrying home among them was 22-year-old Ada James, her destination Clark's Buildings, Union Road, St Philip's. She and her brother Alfred were due to attend the Bible Class tea at the Shaftesbury Crusade. The date was January 27th, 1913.

Plump, dark-haired Ada had become engaged to her long-standing boyfriend, Ted Palmer. Ted, who was 23, was an unstable individual who took a sadistic enjoyment in brandishing a gun to scare his mother and two sisters, with whom he lived in Albany Place, Montpelier.

A faded picture of Ada James.

Ted had experienced a brief spell of glory in the boxing ring and was now finding life as a chair maker somewhat tame by comparison. He had spent almost the whole of 1912 in Canada seeking more conducive employment and had not worked since his return to these shores in early December.

Poverty, however, did not appear to curtail his drinking habits. He had spent much of the Monday in question in various hostelries, arriving at Ada's house in the evening where he waited until she returned at 7.30. The two of them then set out for a walk to Narroways Hill, St Werburgh's, apparently on the best of terms. During their walk, if Ted is to be believed, he mentioned the possibility of leaving in the near future to try his fortune in the West Indies. His plan was that he would send for Ada once he was established.

Ada, who had probably been fed the same line prior to his departure for Canada, reacted to this scheme by throwing her engagement ring at him and saying, 'If you do go I shall go on the town. I've done it before and will do so again.' At this point, according to Ted, 'everything went black'.

The knowledge that his memory rejected was that he savagely slit her throat from ear to ear with a razor and made off towards Ashley Road, where he made attempts at two different shops to purchase writing materials . . . presumably to pen his subsequent suicide note.

This accomplished, he headed for Hodders on the corner of Warwick Road (now the "Ebony" Hair Salon) to obtain laudanum. It was but a brief step to his grandmother's house in Bean Street (a small portion of this thoroughfare remains at the rear of the Greek Orthodox church at the top of Claremont Street; the rest is covered by Easton Way). Here he washed in her back kitchen and, presumably, imbibed the poison.

The police finally caught him, still wandering in the area at 2 a.m. He declined to make a statement other than that he had taken poison. The suicide attempt must have been a half-hearted one as he suffered no serious ill-effects.

The next day he was told that Ada had been found on the corner of Lynmouth Road, having staggered some distance, bleeding to death from a throat wound, and had been taken to the Infirmary where she had later died. 'You don't mean to say she got over that stile?' was Palmer's response. 'Do you think she suffered?'

Ted was then charged with her murder. Before she died Ada had scribbled Ted's name on a scrap of paper and whispered, 'My fiancé did it'.

Edward Henry Palmer was tried on February 19th, 1913. He appeared unmoved as he stood to face the charge, exchanging amicable greetings with his friends in the court. He pleaded not guilty.

Prosecuting Counsel attempted to prove premeditated murder inasmuch as Palmer was carrying a razor newly purchased on the Sunday morning before the crime. His explanation was that he had lost his own razor and evidence put forward by his family would endorse this. His sister had hidden it due to his threatening behaviour. Still, if he had bought the razor on Sunday why was it still in his pocket on Monday night? According to Ted, he was too drunk on the Sunday to shave. It seemed likely that he had it in his mind to frighten Ada.

The jury took just 15 minutes to decide on Palmer's guilt and he was duly hanged.

Ted Palmer was a shallow poseur; one who compensated for his lack of stature by dramatic and empty gestures; his fundamentally unbalanced nature aggravated by alcohol abuse.

Ada was emotional and strong-willed, but failed to understand the effect her impulsive words had on those to whom they were directed.

Throughout the enquiry and subsequent trial there were hints of witnesses having their silence bought. There was also the suggestion that Ada's father was charging the morbidly curious a fee to view his dead daughter's body while it was laid out in the James' front parlour.

The remains of this fearless but misguided girl lie in Greenbank Cemetery.

The spot where Ted Palmer left his fiancée for dead.

'Brandy, Brandy is the cause of it . . .'

The story of William and Alice Hole is a sad one. The couple, who at the time the murder took place had been married for 30 years, were reasonably affluent. They lived in Tower Street, in the parish of Temple, a cobbled thoroughfare leading to Pipe Lane which was swept away for the construction of Temple Way. They employed a servant, Sarah Crocombe, who had been with them for ten years.

In 1874 Hole was 49, his wife a year younger. He was a barge owner engaged on contract work for the railways and had several men working for him. He had been landlord of the quaintly-named "Castle of Comfort", an old hostelry in Tower Street, 20 years earlier, and, during that period, two events took place which could have had a bearing on the final tragic outcome.

Firstly the Holes' only child, a son, was killed. Hole took the loss extremely badly and tried to drown himself in the Float. Then, three years later, he had a serious accident when he was thrown from a gig travelling through St George. His seemingly lifeless body was carried into the nearby Fire Engine public house where, after an hour, he regained consciousness but the severe head injury he received left a legacy of persistent headaches for the rest of his life.

He weathered the storm, however, but gave up the tenancy of the pub in favour of building up a successful barge business. He continued to suffer from bouts of depression, though, and neighbours testified to frequent threats of suicide. One particular night Sarah, the servant, had to physically disarm him as he grabbed a kitchen knife declaring he would 'do away with himself'. He became paranoid about hearing voices, saying 'they were going to get him'. He started drinking fairly heavily and acting strangely. He took to getting up in the middle of the night and going to sleep in another room or sitting downstairs alone, brooding. At other times he would just wander off into the night – where he went no one knew.

Perhaps due to her husband's erratic mood-swings Alice also turned to the bottle. Naturally enough, when both were under the influence arguments would erupt, voices raised in fury and objects thrown.

On August 28th, 1874 William was in a particularly depressive state. He complained of pains in his head and was finding difficulty concentrating on his work. By early evening he had taken recourse to the bottle.

Darkness fell on Tower Street and the residents began to prepare for the night ahead, some to bed, some to work. George Perry, a watchman at Mr Wall's yard patrolled his domain. Henry Merchant, the current landlord of the "Castle of Comfort", called time and started to clear away and lock up. It was a warm evening and Henrietta Dodge at number nine wandered out to her front doorway for a breath of fresh air before retiring to bed with husband John, a painter and decorator.

Jane Morrish, a shoemaker's wife, at number 22 was also thinking about getting ready for bed as was Mary Cotterell at number 17. Her spouse, William, was also employed as a night watchman by Mr Wall.

Sarah, the Hole's long-suffering skivvy, had been out for the evening. At 10.40 p.m. she returned to find Alice, somewhat tipsy, sitting on the front doorstep. Sarah tried to persuade her to go indoors but met with a firm refusal so she went inside for a bite of supper before calling round for a brief word with her brother who lived nearby. On her way back Sarah paused to chat to a neighbour when she recognized Alice's voice screaming and rushed back home.

Henrietta Dodge, meantime, had also witnessed Alice sitting on the doorstep. She had seen William weaving his unsteady way down the street, and at his approach Alice had hastily retreated into the house. Ten minutes later she re-emerged shouting 'You old blackguard!', closely followed by Hole who struck her a sharp blow, and then went back inside locking the door. Alice, feeling more than a little sorry for herself, took herself off to a neighbour's step and moped there awhile before returning to her own doorway. She then became aware of Henrietta and reeled along to number nine. 'I shan't go in tonight,' she confided. If she was looking for sympathy she had picked the wrong person in Henrietta Dodge, who retorted 'You'll be obliged to when the police come round.'

William then unlocked the door and asked his wife to come inside. When she adamantly refused he turned back into the passageway, slamming the door. A few moments elapsed then the door opened again and he repeated his request. 'When I like,' retorted Alice in a fit of bravado.

He struck her again and vanished back into the marital home but was soon back in the street, dealing her a savage knock which sent

Redcliffe Back, where William Hole built up his successful barge business (H. O'Neill, 1822).

her sprawling. He then lunged at her with a knife. She collapsed in a heap in the roadway.

Henrietta, thoroughly alarmed by this time, hastened into her own house but even as she struggled to bolt the door she heard Alice frantically screaming out her name followed by a terrified shriek of 'Murder!'. Heart thudding, Henrietta remained behind her closed door until other shouts of 'Murder!' rent the night air. She opened the door once more and gingerly peered out. The gas lamp outside her house illuminated the whole scene in grim detail. The plump little figure of Alice was propped against the kerb waving her hands helplessly. Blood poured from a great gash in her throat. She could not speak, her windpipe had been severed. Henrietta went completely to pieces but fortunately Jane Morrish and Mary Cotterell were made of sterner stuff. Mary comforted the wounded woman while Jane dashed to the "Castle of Comfort" for towels to staunch the flow of blood. Alice's hand, too, was bleeding profusely. It had been sliced to the bone as she had tried to ward off the attack.

William, meanwhile, was attempting to retrieve the knife which he had flung away after the attack but was frustrated in his efforts by George Perry who had appeared on the scene and Samuel Milsom, a coal runner who lived opposite and worked for Hole. Samuel took charge of the weapon, a kitchen knife with an 8″ blade. It was not particularly sharp so considerable force had been used to inflict such dreadful wounds.

Jane Morrish and Mary carried Alice into her living room and laid her gently on the hearth rug. Jane held the dying woman in her arms as Alice made piteous attempts to speak but her life was fast ebbing away and by the time medical aid arrived it was too late. As her body was borne away to the Infirmary Jane went outside and spoke to William who was leaning against the window sill, arms folded. 'Mr Hole, your wife is dead' she told him, to which he replied, "Brandy, brandy has done it."

He begged Milsom to give him back his knife but Milsom refused. Did he intend to use it on himself?

The police arrived and Hole announced, 'Here I am. I did it. I shall not run away. Take me if you like.'

He asked if he might have a brandy and water before being taken into custody as 'it would be the last he would have for a long time'. This request was refused and he then said 'I know I have done it and shall be hung.'

He was taken to Bedminster Police Station and in spite of being cautioned not to incriminate himself he insisted, 'I cut her throat and here I am.' He raised his chin and made a sweeping movement across his own throat with his hand. 'It was all through a drunken wife,' he told them. 'This has been anticipated these eight months.'

He pleaded to be allowed to go and drown himself and once in the cells he tried to strangle himself with his silk neckerchief. He could not be examined for some days afterwards as he was suffering from delerium tremens and fits.

At his trial the following April, the defence questioned Hole's sanity with a view to making the charge manslaughter but this was overruled and it took the jury a mere ten minutes to reach a verdict of 'Guilty' with no recommendation for mercy. Hole himself seemed to consider the sentence justifiable and went quietly to his death at the gallows later that same month.

It is hard not to feel a certain amount of sympathy with both murderer and victim in this "last straw - heat of the moment" slaying. It is a tale of two people driven apart by grief and, unable to communicate with one another, seeking solace in alcohol. Sadly, as is so often the case, it brought no comfort but instead violence and ultimate tragedy.

A Dastardly Deed in the "Old Castle"

In the 1850s, the Dings was a densely-populated district of Bristol housing working-class people. They were mainly tradesmen, such as John Spear, a shoe-maker. In 1852, he was living in Prince Street with his 32-year-old wife Elizabeth and their four young children.

Elizabeth was a 'clean and industrious' woman who contributed to the family income by engaging in casual work at home. Her husband was not always so industrious. He had a habit of keeping "Saint Mondays" – the nineteenth century equivalent of "a day for the Queen". In other words, when the mood took him, he would abandon his work and spend the day on a tour of local hostelries, often in the company of his brother Abraham, also a married man.

One such day was Tuesday, 19th October 1852. John Spear wheedled some money from his wife early that morning and had begun his drinking session by 9 a.m. The money soon ran out and by lunchtime he had persuaded Abraham to pawn his coat to swell funds. The proceeds from this transaction bought enough drink to last until 3 p.m., when John returned home to coerce Elizabeth to give him more money.

She told him she had none then left the house to visit a sick child in the Infirmary. When she returned home, she discovered that her unscrupulous husband had pawned her two gowns.

Understandably, she was incensed. Her youngest child in her arms, she marched round to her sister-in-law's house and, together, the two women, accompanied by a female friend went in search of their errant spouses.

The inebriated duo were finally run to earth in "The Old Castle", a pub in Castle Street presided over by William Taylor.

Perhaps to give herself Dutch courage, Elizabeth called for three pennyworth of rum out of the remaining fourpence in her purse. She handed the baby to her young companion and approached her husband. She berated him about her missing gowns, crying: 'So help me God, it shall be either for life or death this night.'

John, apparently, became rather subdued at this tirade then he asserted himself and called for another pint of Burton. Elizabeth was furious. 'If you have any more Burton,' she raged, 'I'll break the pint over your head.' So saying, she grabbed a tobacco pipe and threw it at him. It hit him on the head. He took a step towards her and she was seen to crumple into a heap.

At first, onlookers thought she had fainted until someone noticed blood seeping through her garments. As she lay on the inn floor, the life-blood draining from her, her husband cried out: 'Go and fetch a doctor for I know what I have done.'

However, by now Elizabeth was beyond help and she expired from her stab wound as the assembled company, stunned into sobriety, looked on helplessly.

John Spear was tried and transported for life for his heinous crime. But it is not recorded what became of the four little children.

Bustling Castle Street.

Trouble at the "Tennis Court"

November 27th, 1824 was Club Night at the Tennis Court Tavern, Warmley and to the delight of the landlord, William Blatchley and his son John, the place was packed to capacity. However, as the evening wore on and more measures of beer were consumed, old quarrels rose to the surface, old scores had to be settled.

One of the clientele that evening was a waggoner named Isaac Gordon. He also had the somewhat unenviable task of impounding any horses he found roaming on his employer's land. He often found himself in contention with the owners and the previous week one such aggrieved owner was 40-year-old Francis Britton.

Britton was among those present at the Tennis Court on that Saturday night accompanied by some younger members of his clique who, as young men of that type are wont to do, were spoiling for a fight. Thomas Wilmot, 19, was there with 18-year-old Isaac Britton, Samuel Peacock, Robert England, Mark Whiting and James Caines. All of them were familiar to the local magistrates and the Caines family were particularly notorious – every member of the clan had a criminal record and over the past 50 years many had been hanged or transported, their womenfolk included.

With liquor flowing freely and feelings running high, trouble was imminent. It would seem Caines was the original instigator. Was he using Britton's grudge against Isaac Gordon as an excuse to stir up a spot of bother one wonders? He began flicking pieces of a shattered tobacco pipe in Gordon's direction, deliberately trying to rile him. Robert England then joined in, declaring loudly that the man 'deserved a good hiding'. At this, Gordon ran out of patience and he rose from his chair announcing he was off home.

Shortly afterwards Thomas Wilmot too absented himself. It is not clear what happened next but one must assume Wilmot followed Gordon and provoked him, for Isaac Gordon then stumbled back into the inn. Blood was gushing from a split lip. He mumbled that he would stay until his aggressors had left so he could walk home in safety – a misguidedly optimistic view as things turned out.

Perhaps encouraged by Wilmot's display of derring-do the rest of the group were in high spirits. They called for another round of drinks but as Blatchley had called time Robert England purchased six quarts of beer to take away. The mob then made their exit.

By eleven o'clock Isaac deemed it safe to depart. He bid the landlord goodnight and was swallowed up in the darkness of that November night.

The Blatchleys locked up and went off to bed. Less than an hour later they were disturbed by a loud banging at the door. They opened up to a frantic Ben Brittain demanding a light. He had stumbled over a man lying by the roadside a little farther up the road. At first he had taken it to be a drunk but now was convinced the man was dead.

The man, who was, of course, Isaac Gordon, was certainly dead although his body was still warm. He lay in front of the miner's cottage occupied by Edward and Hannah Lewis. The body was taken back to the inn.

Hannah Lewis said she had heard a disturbance outside at around half past eleven as she sat by the dying embers of her fire. Her husband had already retired to bed. The sounds had been a series of heavy thumps and she had thought someone was beating an ass as the blows sounded so forceful. She heard no groans or cries of distress but afterwards she was aware of some loud laughter. When morning dawned Edward discovered a long pole thrust through the hedge which proved to be the Blatchleys' uprooted clothes line post.

At the inquest Mr Watts, a surgeon from Bitton, confirmed the cause of death to be a severe head wound inflicted with a big, broad instrument larger than a stick or bludgeon. He asserted a weapon such as the clothes line post would cause the marks found on Gordon's head. The bones of the skull had penetrated the brain from the right ear down to the neck, and there were two small stab wounds to the forehead. A broken knife had been found near the body.

A verdict of wilful murder by person or persons unknown was returned. The coroner added that the landlord of the Tennis Court should have raised the alarm sooner as, 'from the vigilance of the peace officers living near his home there is little doubt but the murderers would have been apprehended before they separated that night.' As it was the constables, living within a quarter of a mile of the scene of crime were not apprised of the deed until eight o'clock the following morning.

However, as soon as the constables had been advised of events they set about searching for clues, of which there were plenty. In addition to the broken knife, which was proved to have been in the possession of Robert England on that fateful Saturday, there were distinctive footprints, alleged to be those of Caines and the clear print of the seat of a pair of patched trousers identical to those worn by Mark Whiting. These two sets of prints were found in the soft earth in the spot where the post had been dug up.

All seven men were charged with murder at the next Gloucester Assizes but Wilmot was discharged and the two Brittons, Sam Peacock and Robert England were found 'not guilty'. Only James Caines and Mark Whiting were left to face the hangman on April 11th, 1825.

It does seem rather as though these two young men carried the can for the rest of the gang. Although it appears there was sufficient evidence to show they actually procured the murder weapon, what proof was there that either one of them struck the fatal blow? One is left to ponder on the feelings of their confederates on the morning that James Caines and Mark Whiting took that last walk to meet their Maker.

An old photograph of Warmley.

Murder Most Foul . . .

The year was 1812. We were at war with the French as we had been, on and off, since the end of the previous century and would be for a further three years. King George III was suffering increasingly from bouts of madness and the ruling of the country was left mainly in the hands of "Prinnie", the Prince Regent. Lord Liverpool had recently become Prime Minister.

Stokes Croft in Bristol presented a very different image from that of today. The turnpike was still in existence, surrounded by trees and green fields. It was an exclusive area and Daniel Wait, a Lord Mayor of Bristol and a partner in the Castle Bank, had his residence there.

The weather that winter was severe and on the morning of Wednesday, 10th December Mr Wait's coachman had to break the ice covering the pond in order to water the horses.

While doing this, his attention was caught by the sight of a number of crows hovering over a nearby hedge. When they resisted his attempts to drive them away he crossed to the hedge to discover what was attracting them so determinedly to the spot.

To his horror he came upon three small bodies. A newly-born boy and girl had been battered to death, although one had a tape bound twice round its neck, perhaps indicating the strength of its resistance to death.

The third tiny corpse was so mangled and so much of its flesh had been devoured by the birds that not even its sex could be ascertained.

The opinion was formed, by whom records do not indicate, that the three all belonged to one family but it seemed no one could identify them.

The pathetic little bodies were removed to the "Swan" public house which served as a coroner's court and an inquest was carried out the following evening. A verdict of wilful murder by some person or persons unknown was returned.

And there, it would appear, the matter ended. This was, of course, 24 years before the inauguration of the Bristol Police Force. The infant mortality rate was high and, in fact, within the same brief period there were two cases of death by drowning of young, unidentified children without any suspect being apprehended.

But who could have perpetrated such a horrific crime on three small infants? Were they triplets, or twins and an older child, murdered by one, or both, of their parents?

Did their mother die in childbirth and their father, poverty-stricken and deranged with grief, kill them in a frenzy?

There is another possibility. Unmarried mothers in those days would often fall prey to the "baby-farmers" who would take the unwanted child off their hands for a down payment and a fixed weekly sum.

The more unscrupulous of these foster parents would collect the cash and dispose of the baby.

This practice continued throughout the century, the most notorious of this band of flesh traders being Mrs Amelia Dyer who eventually went to the gallows for her crimes after administering fatal doses of laudanum to a frightening number of small charges.

Although the crimes for which she was arraigned took place in the London area she did live for a time in Stapleton, although whether she carried on her nefarious practices there is not known.

So this could be the answer to the mystery – the children placed in the care of a baby-farmer who heartlessly slaughtered them and dumped them in a Stokes Croft hedgerow.

The Savage Sailor

In 1749 the slope from the Downs to Blackboy Hill which now presents a dense cluster of buildings in varying styles of architecture was no more than a series of lanes dotted with tumbledown cottages. At the foot of one of these winding pathways stood the "White Ladies" tavern presided over by a retired seaman, Thomas Symonds and his wife. They employed a servant, 13-year-old Mary Wiltshire, affectionately known as 'Molly'. The couple rented out rooms and among their lodgers was a sailor aged about 40 by the name of Joseph Abseny (or Absemi as some contemporary newspapers spelt it), who apparently came from Sweden. He formed a very strong attachment to Molly and began to lavish rich gifts upon her such as gowns and shifts and silver buckles.

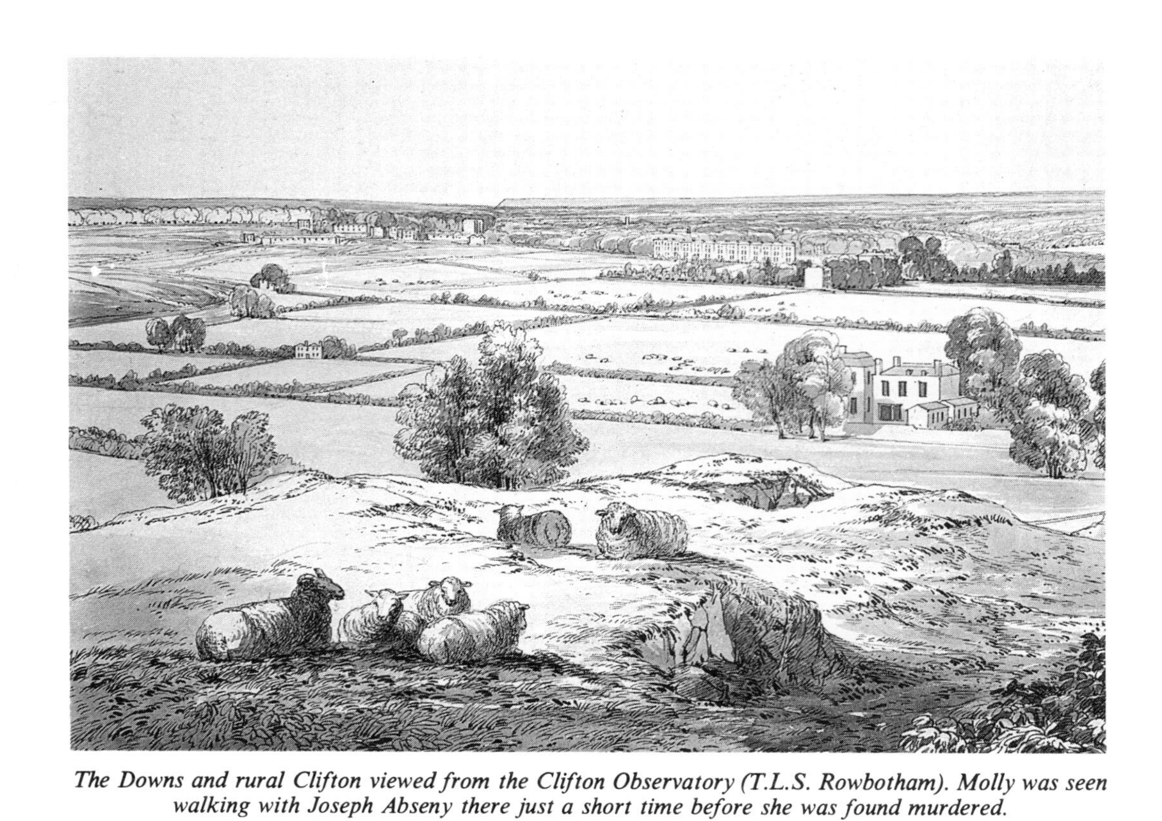

The Downs and rural Clifton viewed from the Clifton Observatory (T.L.S. Rowbotham). Molly was seen walking with Joseph Abseny there just a short time before she was found murdered.

How she reacted to this generosity is not recorded but as she accepted these tokens of his esteem perhaps she was flattered by his attentions, even fond of him. One of their associates described her as 'Abseny's sweetheart'. Nowadays such a liaison would be frowned upon but young girls in those days were in many ways more mature than today's teenagers, being out in the big wide world earning their living at 11 or even younger and some were married by 15.

So what caused the cloud to loom on the horizon? Abseny certainly possessed a very jealous nature and when Molly appeared to wish to extricate herself from the relationship he became extremely verbally abusive and threatening towards her.

One Thursday afternoon, a warm day in July, Mrs Symonds discovered they were running short of butter and asked Molly to go to the "Blackamoor's Head", a nearby inn, to purchase another 3lb. Molly collected a shallow basket from the kitchen and let herself out through the back door. She hurried down the garden path in the sunshine, slipped through the gate at the bottom leading into the lane beyond and proceeded in the direction of Durdham Down, perhaps glad of the excuse to spend a while in the fresh air.

Abseny waited a moment or two then began to follow her. Ann Nurse, a mutual acquaintance, saw them together on the Downs at about this time and noticed he was gripping her by the arm.

Time went by and Mrs Symonds became concerned at the length of time the girl had been absent. She went to look for her. She did not have far to search, stumbling almost immediately on Molly's crumpled body on which had been inflicted the most horrendous injuries. Mrs Symonds guessed at once the identity of the perpetrator of this dreadful deed, remembering seeing Abseny leave the inn so rapidly after Molly's departure. She gazed in disbelief at the mutilated corpse of her little servant. There were nine vicious knife wounds to her head and at one point the blade had passed right through her neck so that there was a wound on either side 'like a slaughtered sheep' to quote the reportage of the day. It seemed she had raised her hand to defend herself and, in doing so, the knife severed her finger at the second joint.

While engaged upon his savage task Abseny himself had sustained a deep gash to the hand and he was unable to stem the flow of blood. The wound bled so copiously that Tom Symonds, together with a hastily gathered band of men, was able to follow the trail of blood with little difficulty.

Absény had taken flight across the Downs and carried on running until he reached Hungroad at Sea Mills where he persuaded the navigator of a pilot boat to row him out to the *Sheerness*, a vessel bound for Cadiz. Unfortunately for Abseny there was not the slightest breeze on that warm July afternoon so he was forced to wait on the deck of the becalmed ship watching his pursuers gain ground by the minute.

Symonds and his posse bound their captive in chains and dragged him off to the Bridewell situated in Lawford's Gate from whence he was taken to Gloucester to await trial, St Judes and, indeed, Clifton being outside the jurisdiction of the city of Bristol in those days.

It is said he faced execution bravely and was filled with remorse and shame at the dreadful result of his obsessiveness. He died after receiving absolution from a Catholic priest on the gallows at Durdham Downs close to the spot where he had so cruelly ended a young girl's life.

The Killing of an Animal Lover

Gertrude O'Leary was a friendly soul, well-liked by everyone in the Stokes Croft area of Bristol where, until her sister Kathleen's death in 1940, the two women had run the "Bell" in Hillgrove Street. She was passionately fond of animals and, as a memorial to her sister, she donated funds to provide an operating theatre at the RSPCA in St James Parade – although sadly the building was destroyed in the blitz the following year.

A devout Catholic, 66-year-old Miss O'Leary attended Mass at St Mary on The Quay where she was acknowledged as a talented pianist, entertaining at social events there.

By 1949 she had established a new business, an off-licence at 13, Thomas Street, directly opposite what is now the Bristol Service Centre. Here she lived quietly with her cats, friends popping in for visits in the afternoon when the shop was closed.

Gertrude O'Leary.

The last day of June that year was fine and sunny. Stokes Croft, somewhat dusty and dilapidated after the bombing it had suffered in the war, was unusually quiet.

The residents of Dalton Square had gone to Weston-super-Mare for the day on their annual outing. Just up the road at the Academy Cinema *The Siren of Atlantis* starred Maria Montez and Jean Pierre Aumont.

At about 10.30 a.m. that Thursday Mrs Metcalfe, who lived at 3, Cox's Buildings, now the site of new flats, glanced out of her front window and saw a 'not very pleasant character' talking to elderly Mrs Brown next door.

Mrs Metcalfe had seen the man around the neighbourhood earlier in the week. He was a short, thin chap aged about 45, dressed in a dirty overcoat, old grey trousers, a tatty trilby and down-at-heel shoes.

Mrs Metcalfe noticed that Mrs Brown looked nervous and called out of the window to her asking what the man wanted. She learned he was looking for rooms. He was well-spoken but with an accent she could not place. She told him there were none available and he moved off in the direction of Stokes Croft.

At 2 p.m. Gertrude O'Leary shut up shop and went through to her living quarters at the back to put her feet up and enjoy a cup of tea with a young neighbour, Mabel Long, sister of the Bristol speedway rider Mike Beddoes.

Mabel left at about 2.30 p.m. Perhaps Gertrude mentioned to her – as she had to another frequent visitor, Pat Fowler of Dalton Square – her unease regarding a short, shabbily-dressed man with a swarthy complexion who had been hanging round the shop of late. Gertrude had confided to Pat she 'did not like the look of him'.

As the afternoon drew on Mrs Elizabeth Sealey, who lived at number 15, was taking advantage of the sunshine out in her backyard.

She heard a stifled scream and shortly afterwards saw a man wearing a trilby hat leave by the rear entrance to Miss O'Leary's shop and walk away across nearby wasteland. She and others were puzzled that the back entrance, usually kept locked, was open that afternoon.

That evening, regulars began queueing up outside the off-licence, perhaps a few banging on the door and calling 'Open up, Gert – it's well gone seven.' But the building remained in darkness. Neighbours began to grow perturbed and eventually one, Fred Dibble, called the police.

When they entered the off-licence at 10.45 p.m., it was to discover Gertrude's body in the ransacked back room. She had been brutally beaten about the head with a flagon beer bottle, then strangled with a cord. A gold watch and a gold pendant set with amethysts and seed pearls were missing from the house.

The next day Bristol CID were sufficiently alarmed to call in Scotland Yard, believing the killer could strike again. That afternoon they took possession of a telegram which had been delivered to 13, Thomas Street, bearing a man's name. They conducted a house-to-house enquiry and soon found a blood-stained suit and trousers in a working men's boarding house close by.

They interviewed a man at Highbridge who had announced in a cafe on the Saturday night that he had been outside the house when the murder was committed.

After such revelations Bristol waited in anticipation of an early arrest – but none took place. Nothing more was heard of the down-at-heel man and the file was placed in the "unsolved" drawer.

If the suspect is still alive he would be in his eighties now. Is there a little old man, somewhere, still trying to reconcile his conscience with the death of a good woman for a couple of trivial trinkets?

Murder in Quiet Redland

Back in 1839 Redland was a pleasant rural area. A feature was Coldharbour Farm, a dairy business run by Mr Warr who delivered milk locally. Various lads worked for him and lodged at the farmhouse.

On the afternoon of Saturday, 9th February, a milkman called Roberts met farm worker John Butt.

He saw him again two hours later – John was lying on a track leading to the farm. He had been very badly beaten and was very weak.

Roberts ran to tanner James Knowly's house on the Redland boundary for help, and between the two of them, they managed to carry the badly-injured man to the Black Boy Inn. There they were joined by another man who helped them take the youngster to the Infirmary.

John Butt died of his horrific injuries four days later – but before he died he managed to make a statement to the police.

He told how he had been cutting hay in one of Warr's fields and carrying it to the cow shed. It was when he was stacking the hay that he was approached by one of Farmer Warr's former hands, William Davis. The two knew each other and had once shared lodgings. They had never quarrelled.

'This is good hay, is it not?' Davis said, but Butt told him 'I don't know' and was keen to end the conversation so he could lock up. Davis took the hint and began to stroll up Redland Lane. After locking up, Butt caught up with him saying, 'Well, William, what are you up to?' Davis made no reply, just stared into space across the meadow. Butt continued up the lane – and then Davis chased after him and brutally attacked him with what is believed to have been a hammer. As Butt lay helpless on the ground Davis stole his watch and chain on which he wore a four pence piece he had drilled through for the purpose.

Davis was arrested and gradually the truth of what had happened emerged as he confessed to fellow prisoners.

After attacking his former workmate, he made off with his watch, buried the fob and keys, washed his bloodstained clothes and walked into town. He pledged the watch for £1 at a pawnbrokers in Castle Street giving his name as George Smith. He walked to St

James' Back and bought pork and a quart of ale. As he was walking back up towards Redland, he met a girl he knew. 'Where have you been? Haven't you heard there's a man with his brains nearly beaten out?' she said. Davis said he had no idea what she was talking about, turned on his heel and went back to town. He treated himself to a new shirt and boots, then returned to St James' Back for a portion of faggots and potatoes before setting off to wander through Horfield and Filton.

At about 1.30 a.m. he reached Patchway in the pouring rain and a local man invited him in for a cup of tea and some bread and butter.

Fortified, he continued his journey to New Passage where a plain clothes policeman arrested him and marched him to Clifton Police Station. Davis tried to hide damning evidence by throwing his pawn ticket down the privy, but it was a useless act. The police had their man – and they knew it.

Police Inspector Attwood confronted him with the words, 'I would rather see your face than the prettiest girl's in Bristol!' At the subsequent trial the jury unanimously found him guilty. Davis, described by a reporter as a 'fresh-faced country lad', remained calm throughout the trial. When he heard the verdict, he announced, 'I have nothing to say'. He was hanged at Gloucester on April 6th.

The murder appears to have been committed on impulse. The only possible motives were jealousy of young Butt's secure situation on the farm or simple greed, with the robbery's proceeds spent on an evening's pleasure in Bristol.

But William Davis's freedom was short-lived . . . and his capture and death was inevitable.

The Black Boy Inn.

Death on a Busy Morning

It may be easier for older Bristolians who can remember College Green before the lowering of the green and the building of the Council House to imagine the elegance of the place in the eighteenth century.

It was in the middle of the eighteenth century, at around the time of George III's accession to the throne, that building development accelerated noticeably in the city. By the 1760s plans were under way for the creation of a floating harbour and the wealthy merchants of the city had begun to build their houses away from the crowded areas of Temple and the Quays.

Chic residences began to appear on the airy slopes of Clifton, the building of King Square commenced in 1740 and the lower section of Park Street sprang up as a terrace of beautifully designed houses. On the western edge of the green lay College Street, consisting of rather more modest dwellings with bow windows.

In 1764 one of the houses in the shadow of the Cathedral was occupied by James and Frances Ruscombe and their servant, Mary Sweet, also known as Champness.

On Thursday, 27th September of that year there was the usual mid-morning bustle of activity in the area, with worshippers hurrying to College prayers. It is therefore surprising, in view of the busyness of the scene, that an intruder could enter the Ruscombes' house, carry out an awful crime and leave unnoticed.

It was not until midday that the crime was discovered. A relative calling at the house for a luncheon appointment was met with a gruesome sight. The body of Frances Ruscombe lay sprawled on the staircase, her face horribly mutilated. There were vicious wounds to her mouth, her throat had been cut, one eye had been completely beaten out and her skull had been shattered by a heavy blow which had penetrated her brain.

In the back parlour lay the corpse of Mary, the servant. Her throat had been slashed with such force as to almost sever the head from her body; her jaw was broken and her forehead had been subjected to a fierce attack, apparently by a hammer. A deep wedge-shaped cleft to the skull had been dealt by her killer. Both bodies were still warm and medical men thought they had been dead two hours at the most.

Bristol Cathedral and the High Cross as it was in the mid-eighteenth century in this painting by Samuel Scott. The peace and quiet of elegant College Green was shattered one morning in 1764 when Frances Ruscombe and her maid were brutally murdered in their home.

Some of the rooms had been searched and a portmanteau ransacked. 57 guineas were stolen from one source and a silver purse with 36 shilling pieces and 21 guineas was also missing.

Many arrests were made, and a prime suspect was a baker with the strange name of Peacable Robert Matthews. Just why he came under suspicion is not clear although he had been in trouble in the past, some eight years prior to the murder for selling underweight bread. He had been prosecuted by the Baker's company and fined £6.12s.6d.

A number of rewards were offered for information which could help solve the shocking crime. The M.P. for Bristol at the time, Robert Nugent (later Viscount Clare), offered £500, while Mr Elton, the Town Clerk, posted a notice offering £100 in an attempt to bring the murderer to justice. Frances' own family – her sisters Elizabeth and Sarah Jefferies and husband James – offered rewards of £50 and £10 respectively. All was to no avail, however. The perpetrator was never apprehended.

Thomas de Quincey, that noted man of letters, learned the details of the crime on a visit to Bristol and became fascinated by the case. He makes reference to it in his famous essay "Murder as One of the Fine Arts". His account of the affair (*The English Mail Coach*) varies from the newspaper reports of the day. In his version a neighbour forces an entrance and finds the body of Frances Ruscombe in her bedroom and the maid's corpse on the stairs. He dismisses the two main suspects – the baker and a chimney sweep – as being unequal to such a crime, and is convinced the culprit was a Lancashire highwayman who was hanged for robbery some years later. Apparently the man, whose body was destined for use in a medical school, was cut down before he died and he recovered on his way to the dissecting room for long enough to confess to the murder.

This theory, according to de Quincey, was endorsed by a Lancashire woman who was one of the highwayman's neighbours. She had told de Quincey that the man in question was absent from the locality for a fortnight during the time the murder was committed. When he returned there appeared a deluge of dollars in the district and Mrs Ruscombe was reputed to have 'hoarded about 2000 of that coin'.

The house where the slaughter of the two women had occurred was shunned forever afterwards and no one could be persuaded to take on the tenancy. It was demolished in the early part of the following century and re-built by Sir Jarrit Smith.

A Drunken Deed in St Leonard's Lane

Nowadays when referring to the Port of Bristol one naturally thinks of Avonmouth, finding it hard to visualize a time when the Tramways Centre was the hub of maritime commerce and the sails of the tall ships could be glimpsed through the buildings of Baldwin Street and Clare Street. This was the spectacle which so fascinated H. V. Morton that he wrote of it in his book *In Search of England.*

In the eighteenth century the Quays were populated by ship's chandlers and the cobbled streets teemed with sailors from all over the world. Taverns and bawdy houses abounded in the area to cater for, and cash in on, the tastes of these nautical men.

Eleanor Diller (or Dillard, the name by which she is referred to by some contemporary writers) was well known in the dens of iniquity of quayside Bristol in the 1740s. She hailed from a northern port, hence her nickname of 'Liverpool Nell' and 1748 found her resident in a house of ill-fame in Fisher Lane behind Queen Square.

On the night of November 12th, 1748 things got a little out of hand at this establishment. Young Jeremiah Hayes was out on the town with two companions and all had clearly imbibed rather too much liquor than was good for them. It is not recorded what sparked off the dispute between Jeremiah and Liverpool Nell but some remark or gesture obviously incensed him and he threw her to the floor. His anger accelerated and he grabbed her by her hair and dragged her across the room, swearing he 'would be the death of her that night.' She managed to haul herself to her feet and, frightened by Jeremiah's fury made her escape by the back door into St Leonard's Lane. Realizing she was being pursued she screamed out 'Murder!' but her cries were ignored, perhaps because girls of her profession were expected to be able to take care of themselves. Events become a little confused at this point but it would seem the protagonist and his confederates caught up with her, bundled her into a sack and flung her into the dark icy waters flowing towards Bristol Bridge.

The next morning her inert body was found lying face down in the mud of the river bank. She must have managed to struggle free of the sack but her strength failed and, encumbered by the voluminous clothes of the day, the river claimed her life before she could pull herself to safety. Several marks of violence could be seen on her body.

Jeremiah Hayes was arrested and although he protested he had not killed her a charge of wilful murder was brought against him. There emerges little proof that Jeremiah Hayes was the sole perpetrator of the crime but for some reason his unnamed companions got off Scot free.

H. O'Neill's watercolour drawing of St Leonard's Lane where 'Liverpool Nell' met her fate.

Slain by her Servant

At five o'clock in the morning on March 3rd, 1849 Mrs Fry was awakened by screams which seemed to emanate from the bedroom of the house next door in Trenchard Street. Mrs Ham, her lodger, was also disturbed by the commotion. The two women agreed the cries were coming from the first floor front room where their neighbour, Miss Elizabeth Jefferies, a woman in her sixties, slept. Mrs Fry instructed Mrs Ham to bang on the wall with a stick and when she did so the noises ceased and the two women were able to resume their interrupted repose.

At seven o'clock there came a knock on the door. A young girl stood on the step and introduced herself as Miss Jefferies' servant. She said she had been sent round to apologise for the earlier disturbance. A cat had jumped on Miss Jefferies' bed, terrifying her and causing her to scream, the girl explained. 'You must have thought we were killing each other,' she smiled.

This was the first time the neighbours had met Sarah Harriet Thomas, the latest in a long line of servants employed by the woman so disagreeable by nature that even her own brother, with whom she once shared a house, never visited her.

She did have one friend, however, and that was Mrs Susan Miller. Mrs Miller had called on her the previous afternoon, a Friday, and had promised to visit again on the Saturday. When she duly arrived at 6, Trenchard Street she found the house closed up and no amount of banging at the door could evoke any response.

Earlier in the morning, though, a little before lunch time, some form of activity had been witnessed at number 6. George Webb, a porter who lived across the street watched a young woman, whose description tallied with that of 19-year-old Sarah, and a man removing objects from the house. The two of them walked off in the direction of St Michael's Hill. A bundle was deposited at a confectioner's in Magdelen Lane to be called for later.

Between half past three and four o'clock that afternoon, Sarah turned up at her parent's home in Horfield. It appears that George and Ann Thomas asked no questions about her arrival out of the blue, nor about the luggage they were requested to carry in.

That evening Sarah returned to Bristol and met a cab driver she knew, a Mr Thomas Rowley. She persuaded him to collect a bundle she had left at a nearby confectionery shop, and then she returned home, arriving at half past nine.

Although she spent the whole of the following day at her parents' home it would appear they didn't quiz her at all about the possessions she had brought with her which included jewellery, silverware and cash – a story the police found hard to swallow for when they arrested Sarah they took her mother into custody at the same time.

Sarah travelled into Bristol on the Monday, Tuesday and Wednesday evenings but, her mother said, she always returned early and 'with no one from this house' which is not exactly the same as saying she came home alone. It is clear that Sarah had proved troublesome to her parents in the past. She had left several positions abruptly and, in each case, money and certain objects had disappeared with her.

On Wednesday, 7th March Elizabeth Jefferies' body was found. She was lying in her bedchamber with brutal wounds to her head. A large blood-stained stone lay nearby. It later transpired it was one she used to prop open the kitchen door. The body of Miss Jefferies' dog was discovered in the back yard.

At ten o'clock that night the police went in search of the missing servant girl. She was finally run to earth crouched in the coal hole under the stairs of her parents' cottage. The little dwelling was combed minutely, even to the extent of rousing her father from his sick bed. The booty soon came to light – bracelets, brooches, a ring, a gold chain, old coins (principally half-franc pieces), part of a silver buckle, 27 sovereigns, 4 half-sovereigns, 15s.4d in silver and 2¾d in copper were discovered. Most incriminating of all was a spoon and sugar tongs engraved with the initials 'E.J.'

Sarah was arrested, as was her mother, who stated at this point 'I won't tell any more lies for her.'

Initially Sarah tried to implicate Miss Jefferies' brother but, finding herself skating on thin ice, she produced a tale of a former servant who turned up on that Saturday morning. Sarah alleged she saw the girl as she put up the bedroom shutters. In a statement made to the police she quoted the ex-servant as saying:

'I have lived here as a servant and sent several after my character [i.e. attempted to obtain references] but they would get none. Now I will go and give her her breakfast.' Sarah went on to describe her as 'having a stone in her hand with her and going upstairs with it. I went up an hour after and saw her folded up in the bedclothes; she then got the keys, gave me thirty sovereigns, seven or eight rings and ever so many brooches. I left there a little after one o'clock leaving the other servant behind me; she said she would lock the door and there could never be anything found out about me. I don't know if they have found the dog; it is in the water closet.'

Exhaustive attempts were made to trace this elusive former servant whose name, said Sarah, was either Maria Lewis or Maria Williams. Susan Miller had vague recollections of a girl whom Miss Jefferies had employed in the not-too-distant past but thought her name was Rebecca. Agencies that had supplied domestic staff to Miss Jefferies were unable to help and a blank was drawn. A name could not be conjured up to fit this young maid.

The last servant before Sarah who could positively be identified was Lucy Chad, a sixteen-year-old from Bath. Both she and her mother were cross-examined carefully. After recovering from an illness Lucy had come to Bristol to find herself work while staying with her aunt, Mrs Lewis, in Avon Street. She was engaged by Miss Jefferies, and started work at the Trenchard Street house on the Thursday before Christmas. Lucy remained there five weeks until January 24th when her health began to fail again as a consequence, she said, of the somewhat harsh treatment she received at Miss Jefferies' hands.

Sarah took up her position on February 5th so this leaves two weeks unaccounted for. Was the mysterious Rebecca or Maria employed there during this fortnight?

At this point a totally new story came to light, one told by young Mary Sullivan a nine-year-old girl who led her blind uncle, John Collins round the pubs by night where he played the fiddle to eke out his three shillings a week parish relief money. This girl lived with her uncle at the back of the "Ship" in Steep Street and knew Sarah quite well, testifying that the servant had been 'keeping company with a rifleman' for at least a month before the murder. Mary informed the court that on the fateful Saturday, she was downstairs in the "Flitch of Bacon", an inn in Host Street, with her uncle. Also present was a young man called Matthew Lyon and two riflemen, one of whom was Sarah's beau. Mary claimed the group were plotting the murder of Miss Jefferies. Around midnight, after a few drinks, Matthew and one of the other men climbed over the wall which separated the hostelry from the yard of 6, Trenchard Street. Unseen by the men,

Mary and her uncle followed through a doorway in the wall and crept up to the house where Mary witnessed Lyon strike Miss Jefferies on the forehead while the other man hit her with the side of his sword. Lyon then killed the dog, took it downstairs to the yard and flung it away.

Mary's account was unreliable – it would appear ridiculous that the men climbed over a 20ft high wall when they could have simply passed through the doorway as Mary and her uncle did. She was also very vague about the geography of the house. But why would she tell such a tale? Was she merely a sensation seeker?

Sarah Harriet Thomas.

With Lucy Chad's evidence, Sarah's story regarding the embittered ex-servant seems highly unlikely. In Lucy's description of life in the Jefferies' household she deposed that her mistress slept with the house keys in her bedroom and that all doors and shutters were carefully secured each night. Miss Jefferies herself was the one to open up in the mornings. How then was Sarah able to admit the ex-employee?

Steps leading from Trenchard Lane to Host Street (drawing by T.L.S. Rowbotham). Young Mary Sullivan claimed that a plot to murder Miss Jefferies was hatched in a tavern in Host Street, but her eye-witness account was later discredited.

The house keys themselves were discovered on the Wednesday after the murder. They were spotted in a groove on a window ledge at the "Flitch of Bacon" when William Vickery, who was resident there, was putting up the shutters. Had they lain there since the day of the slaying and, if so, why had he not noticed them before? The keys were handed to Mary Price, the landlord's wife who had, in turn, passed them on to the police. She denied knowing Mary Sullivan but had heard she was 'not quite in her senses' but, she added 'they are such a bad lot you can't believe them.' She did not elucidate further.

During the initial hearing Sarah had not endeared herself to judge and jury by 'behaving with levity' but by the time she was tried the dire consequences became real to her. When the judge pronounced her 'Guilty' and sentenced her to death she broke down completely and she was dragged screaming to the gallows.

Was her account a complete tissue of lies or is it possible she was manipulated by others? We shall never know.

The contemporary crime reporter E. Austin, who attended the execution, expressed the view that the confession that was finally forced out of her was made for, and not by, her. 'How much of it she understood is a matter on which I will not venture to speculate,' he wrote in his "Anecdotage" several years after the event. He spoke with contempt of her 'friends' who were in a great state of excitement on the morning of the hanging, enquiring of their neighbours if they were going to 'see our Sal hung'. He tells how, when her lifeless body was swinging in the April breeze 'ribald jests were bandied about; and, after waiting to see the corpse cut down, the crowd dispersed, and the harvest of the taverns in the neighbourhood commenced.'

A Baby's Frozen Tears

The year 1802: George III was on England's throne. Elegant houses were being built in Clifton and Jane Austen's contemporaries were taking the waters at Hotwells Spa.

On the frosty Wednesday morning of January 20th, 14-year-old William Reeves and his friend James Biggs set off up Charlotte Street towards Brandon Hill intending to shoot sparrows. They climbed over the stile and set off up a footpath. They spotted a robin and decided to aim for it, but at this point their attention was caught by a basket lying about four or five yards from the path. The two youths investigated its contents. Squashed inside was the body of a toddler, scantily clad in a short garment with a cloth over its face.

Alarmed, they went for assistance and encountered a gardener in Great George Street who returned with them to Brandon Hill. He used a stick to push the cloth away from the child's face. Its tongue was hanging out of its mouth and had turned black. Tear-drops had frozen like beads on the baby boy's cheeks and his fists were clenched in helpless pain.

The gardener sent them off to St Peter's Hospital and they reported the incident to Bracey the doorkeeper there. He arranged for the tiny corpse to be taken to the Council House and from there it was taken to St Peter's Hospital to await an inquest. Among the baby's clothing was a woman's glove.

On the Sunday two women were apprehended and committed for trial. They were Maria Davis, the victim's 20-year-old widowed mother, and her friend Charlotte Bobbett. Maria's husband, a soldier, had been killed in Ireland just after the baby Richard's birth. She had recently been in receipt of a charitable donation of 3s 6d per week from a Miss Phillips in Clifton to put the child out to nurse, but after a couple of weeks the nurse, Mary Robertson, received no further contributions and on January 15th brought the child to the Sugar Loaf Inn in Bridewell Lane and handed him back to Maria.

Maria, in the meantime, had struck up a friendship with Charlotte at the "Kings Arms" in Baldwin Street. She had also made the acquaintance of another woman, a market trader called Susanna Avard, and approached her one day saying she had no lodgings, money or food. She begged to be allowed to stay at her home in New Street, St Philip's. Susanna took pity on her and Maria arrived on

An early nineteenth century lithograph from a sketch by S.T. Davis. This view of Bristol is seen from Brandon Hill, where Maria left her little boy.

Saturday, 16th January, together with her little boy.

Maria fed the baby, put it to bed and went out, not returning until midday on the Sunday. She brought Charlotte back with her. The following evening the two girls went out, taking the boy with them. They went to the "Neptune" in Bath Street.

Maria had already confessed to Charlotte that the baby was a great burden to her. Charlotte suggested they convey the hapless infant to Redcliffe churchyard and leave it there in the hope someone would take it in. When they reached the churchyard Maria began to have misgivings, fearing that dogs would devour the baby. They continued on to Mayor's Paddock at the foot of Redcliffe Hill and left the boy there for a while. He cried so violently that they were obliged to pick him up again and walk on to Redcliffe Mead. Again they left young Richard but returned in answer to his cries.

Walking on they met two men carrying guns. It was, by now, three in the morning. Maria told them the sorry tale of her poverty and the men gave her what money they had in halfpennies. The women then returned to Susanna's house.

On the Tuesday evening between six and seven o'clock, the two girls took the boy out again, borrowing Susanna's market basket. Charlotte carried the boy as far as the Drawbridge, then Maria took over, walking up Park Street to Brandon Hill.

Maria had formed the conclusion that someone in one of the big houses nearby would hear his cries and rescue him. He was crying when they put him in the basket so she fetched some sugar and put it in a cloth over his mouth, to quieten him sufficiently for them to make their escape.

It is not clear whether the girls returned to Susanna's house, though it seems unlikely. But on their next encounter Maria explained she had put the child with a nurse. Susanna asked what had become of her basket and Maria assured her she would buy her a new one as a replacement.

They next met up on Bristol Bridge on the Friday. Susanna asked her if the baby found dead of exposure on Wednesday was hers. 'Oh no,' said Maria, explaining her child had been put in St Peter's Hospital. They went together to Mr Johnstone's in Temple Street and then Maria confessed what she had done.

Meanwhile Mary Robertson had identified the pathetic little soul and the two girls were taken into custody, where they apparently quite readily told their stories.

The Park Street surgeon, Mr David Davies, who carried out the post mortem, said he had found no marks of violence on the child. It was 15 months old at the time of its death. It had been late in cutting its teeth. It was suffering from a bowel disease and had died in a spasm of pain.

The jury were united in their verdict of guilty.

Before Maria met her inevitable fate at the gallows she said to her confederate: 'My dear Charlotte, do you forgive me? I hope you do not die in enmity with me.' To which Charlotte replied, 'No, I die in peace with man-kind and I hope when we are turned off an angel will come and receive our souls.'

After their bodies were cut down they were taken to the infirmary and dissected for the training of medical students.

Death in Leigh Woods

The Clifton Suspension Bridge is probably Bristol's most recognisable landmark. It is difficult to imagine the Avon Gorge without it, yet in 1857, the year in which this story is set, work on it had reached a standstill. Money to finance the project had run out after the twin towers were built and serious doubts were being expressed as to whether it would ever be completed.

In the 1850s Leigh Court was the home of William Miles, M.P. Among his extensive staff he employed a gamekeeper, George Worts. On the morning of Friday, 11th September 1857 Worts, going about his usual business on the estate, came across what appeared to be a large patch of blood and on examining the stain more closely he found that an attempt had been made to cover the blood with clumps of mould. He then spied some footprints leading to the cliff's edge. He followed them, peered down below, then saw, to his horror, what appeared to be the body of a woman in a crumpled heap. He quickly retraced his steps and sought the help and moral support of his friend Sage. Together they hastened to

Ashton police station, bringing back with them Superintendent Jones who made a detailed on-the-spot investigation of the body before having it removed to the Rownham Inn to await an inquest.

The woman, thought to be in her twenties, had a bullet hole in the right side of her head and her throat had been slashed twice with such force that her head was almost severed from her body. She was attired in a dark grey alpaca dress trimmed at the neck and down the bodice with white lace. A pocket had been cut away from her dress, presumably in case it contained effects which might aid rapid identification. The murderer had, however, overlooked one vital clue. On the grass lay a lace-trimmed handkerchief embroidered with the initials 'C.P.'

There was a delay in arranging the inquest – the coroner resided at Cheddar and it took a while to make contact with him – but in the meantime handbills were produced and circulated in an attempt to solve the mystery. A photograph was taken of the corpse and the body was placed on display. People flocked to the viewing, many out of morbid curiosity rather than a genuine wish to help the police identify the body.

Meanwhile the cut away pocket had been discovered on the perimeter of the Smythe estate by a gamekeeper called Fry. It had been weighted down with a stone and flung over the boundary wall.

A careful scrutiny was made of the dead woman's clothing in the hope it would offer some clue as to who she was. Her stays were found to have been made by Goodmans of Stall Street, Bath. Staff recalled the purchaser as being a young woman who told them she lived near Saltford, was shortly to be married and thereafter emigrate to America. A laundress in the employ of the Hon. Mrs Hutchinson of Dorset House, Clifton thought the clean, neat undergarments were marked in a similar fashion to those of a girl who had been in employment there some while previously. Further evidence was obtained from a local dressmaker, Mary Jane Kelston, who recognised her workmanship in the outfit the dead woman wore.

All this information led the police to a house in Freshford, near Bath, the residence of Mr S. G. Bythesea where it was confirmed a young woman answering the description by the name of Charlotte Pugsley had indeed been in service there but had left the previous Wednesday in the company of an old friend of hers, one John Beale, her possessions packed in three boxes.

The hunt, then, was on for John Beale, a native of Long Ashton.

It was established that, at the time of the murder, he was employed as a butler by Captain Watkins of Badby House, Daventry, Northants and he had gone to his employer some days previously with a request for compassionate leave. He explained that his father had met with a serious accident at work and when the news had been conveyed to the family home his sister had collapsed from shock and later died. Captain Watkins gave his permission at once and Beale left Daventry on Sunday, 6th September. He reached Bristol the following day where he met a cousin of his called Wood.

On the Wednesday morning Beale informed his cousin he was going on a visit to Bath. By the afternoon he had arrived at Freshford where he collected Charlotte and the three large boxes which comprised her luggage. They were labelled "Mr Beale, passenger to Bristol. To be left until called for." He deposited them at Limpley Stoke station and then he and Charlotte set off for Bristol. Several acquaintances of his verified they had seen him in the city at different times on the Thursday accompanied by a woman.

John William Beale was arrested soon after his return to Daventry. He was found to have in his possession two pocket pistols, one loaded and one recently discharged, and a bloodstained clasp knife. There was, too, blood on the wristband of his shirt. Two of Charlotte's boxes were found in his bedroom, the third had been concealed in the cellar. He told police they belonged to his sister. Of Charlotte's silk dress there was no trace. It later transpired Beale had already made a present of it to another of his lady friends.

Beale's statement was a somewhat garbled and contradictory account. He said that he had accompanied Charlotte to Bristol, at her request, on the day in question. He admitted that he had had a long-standing friendship with her but stressed it was platonic and was always ready to lend her money or help her in any way he could. He claimed that she had been married before and was to wed again. He alleged that on Thursday, 10th September he had escorted her from Freshford to Bristol where they met her intended at the railway station. The fiancé and Charlotte went off together, and Beale claimed that was the last he saw of them. He eventually returned to Daventry on Saturday.

His statement was dismissed and it then emerged that Beale was a married man.

At the initial enquiry a number of witnesses swore to having seen Beale walking in the direction of Leigh Woods in the company of a woman who fitted Charlotte's description, while others testified to seeing him returning alone. The key witness for the Prosecution was Louisa Ford, housekeeper to Mr Bythesea. She had known Charlotte for two years and was under the impression that Beale had been courting Charlotte for a number of years, since 1850 to the best of her belief. Charlotte had confided to Louisa that she and Beale were to be married in Southampton, before emigrating to the United States, but they had first to visit Bristol as Beale had some business to attend to there.

The trial of John William Beale took place at Bourton, Somerset in December 1857 and after the verdict went against him, a crowd of nearly 10,000 watched him hang on January 12th, 1858.

After Beale's death, E. Austin, a contemporary crime reporter who had covered the case for his paper, published a confession alleged to have been made by Beale. In it the condemned man described how he and Charlotte left a coffee shop in Temple Street late on the Thursday afternoon and made their way up to Nightingale Valley.

They spent hours there, walking and talking, eventually coming to sit on the grass by the cliff top. It was a warm evening and Charlotte removed her bonnet and cloak, spreading the latter on the ground to use as a blanket. Beale was smoking. It was then, according to him, that she began to pressurise him to leave his wife and travel with her to America. An argument ensued and he lost his temper. In his words 'She came to clip me round because I was in such a rage, to kiss and cool my passion.' It was then he pulled out his pistol and shot her. She fell back, holding her handkerchief to her face and lay on the ground groaning. Panic-stricken the noise would attract a passer-by he drew a razor from his pocket and slit her throat. He then rolled her body over the cliff's edge and waited there a short while. Hearing no sound from her, he assumed she was dead and started taking precautions that the body should not be identified. He cut the pocket away from the cloak as she had been shopping that morning and he was afraid it might contain receipts which could be traced. 'There were only two or three shillings in her pocket,' he said, 'so someone else must have had her money, as most likely she had it in her stays or bosom.' He then gathered some mould from a near-by mole-hill to cover up the bloodstains. He overlooked the handkerchief but crumpled up the bonnet and pushed it into his pocket and rolled up the cloak to carry under his arm. He disposed of the pocket then went back down the valley where he washed his hands and the razor in the river. By this time it was midnight. He left the cloak on one of the iron posts which supported the chains on the side of Cumberland Basin, just past the Cumberland Hotel. He continued on towards Trinity Church, making for the Casino but when he arrived there they were on the point of closing so he took himself off in the direction of Marsh Street where he spent the night at the London Chop House in the company of a man named Hawkins.

All in all a puzzling case in spite of the wealth of detail available. Just what was Beale's motive? It seems all far too carefully planned to be a heat of the moment crime as Beale would have us believe.

Beale himself emerges as a cad of the first order, persuasive, with a manner convincing enough to gull Captain Watkins with his far-fetched tale of his sister's demise and a cool individual, too, one must conclude, for him to consider a visit to the Casino only hours after slaying his girlfriend. But Charlotte herself? She remains a total enigma. Was she really aware her suitor was a married man as he claimed? She gave no hint to Louisa Ford that he was married and no indication is given by anyone, except Beale, that she was anything but a moral and respectable girl, fastidious in her dress with her silk gowns, kid boots, fine petticoats and speckled straw bonnet.

So there seem to be two possibilities – either she sincerely believed he had honourable intentions but had perhaps begun to hint that after seven years their relationship should be elevated to a more permanent footing. Maybe he decided to play along with her, lure her to some lonely spot and dispose of her. Otherwise we have to accept Beale's story that she was a conniving temptress out to seduce him away from his wife and that he killed her in a fit of temper. Somehow the former explanation seems to ring more true.

Right: *An early nineteenth century view (by Samuel Jackson) of the Avon Gorge, with Rownham Ferry, the old Hotwell House and Windsor Terrace.*

More Bristol Books

Redcliffe Press have now published more than 100 books about the city. Here is a selection.

Loxton's Bristol: A city's Edwardian years in black and white by Samuel Loxton £4.95
A selection of Loxton's black and white drawings which are marvellous exercises in nostalgia, not only for buildings which in many cases have since disappeared but for the evocation of a leisurely age before the motor car.

Offbeat Bristol by James Belsey £2.95
A selection of stories that will astonish, amuse, sadden and fascinate everyone who knows and loves the city – and provide a suitably 'offbeat' introduction to visitors.

A Bristol Panorama by Doreen Street £4.99
An amazing collection of anecdotes about characters, events and little known places from the Bristol of yesterday.

Bristol & Co. by Helen Reid £4.95
A history of old established Bristol firms – from butchers to stockbrokers.

Bristol Between the Wars by David Harrison £4.95
Bristol seen through the eyes of those who lived through two decades of change, richly illustrated with contemporary photographs.

Bedminster Boy: A childhood remembered by Leonard Vear £3.95
The story of childhood during the Depression, and the years leading up to the 1939–45 war.

Bristol: Beyond the Bridge by Michael Manson £4.95
The turbulent story of Redcliffe, Temple and St. Thomas from the Middle Ages to today.

Bristol Observed by J.H. Bettey £4.95
Innumerable visitors to Bristol have recorded their reactions to the city from famous observers like Cromwell and J.B. Priestley to the lesser known, such as Elizabethan soldiers and itinerant preachers.

Bristol in the Fifties edited by James Belsey £4.95
Bristol's best writers recall life in Bristol as it was around 40 years ago.

Bristol Suburban by Mike Oakley £4.95
Comprehensive study of the city's railway network, which is now mostly disused, and a brief history of each station and halt.

The Forgotten Front: Bristol at War 1914–1918 by James Belsey £3.50
This book presents a rare picture of the full tragic impact of the Great War on the city.

Images of Bristol by James Belsey & David Harrison £5.95
A selection of Victorian and Edwardian photographs showing life in Bristol in the nineteenth century.

Siren Nights compiled by the Rev. Paul Shipley £3.50
This collection of eye witness accounts shows how Bristolians faced up to the constant threat of death and destruction during the blitzes.

West at War by James Belsey and Helen Reid £5.95
Personal stories of life during the Second World War from Bristol, Bath, Weston-super-Mare, Gloucestershire and Somerset.